CHRISTMAS IN BIAFRA

AND OTHER POEMS

CHRISTMAS IN BIAFRA
AND OTHER POEMS

BY CHINUA ACHEBE

ANCHOR BOOKS
DOUBLEDAY & COMPANY, INC.
GARDEN CITY, NEW YORK
1973

Acknowledgments

The poem "Mango Seedling" was first published in the *New York Review of Books* and was dedicated to the memory of the poet Christopher Okigbo, in 1968. "Those Gods Are Children" first appeared in a somewhat different form in *The Conch;* "Love Song (for Anna)" in *Zuka* and "Their Idiot Song" in *Transition.* A good number of the others have appeared in *Okike,* the new journal of African writing.

FIRST ANCHOR EDITION PUBLISHED SIMULTANEOUSLY
WITH HARDCOVER, 1973,
BY DOUBLEDAY & COMPANY, INC.

ISBN: 0-385-00840-6
ANCHOR BOOKS EDITION: 1973

To the Memory of My Mother

CONTENTS

GODS, MEN AND OTHERS

EPILOGUE

Preface

In 1971 my first volume of poetry was published in Nigeria by
Nwankwo-Ifejika of Enugu. It was called *Beware, Soul Brother
and other poems*. There were altogether twenty-three poems in
that volume. I have retained them all here although some have
been revised, a few re-written completely and one given a brand
new name. In addition, there are seven later poems bringing the
total in the present volume to thirty, a more rounded and, to my
mind, more restful number than twenty-three. I have also re-
grouped the entire work into five sections that have suggested
themselves to my mind.

Chinua Achebe
Nsukka, March 1972

PROLOGUE

1966

absent-minded
our thoughtless days
sat at dire controls
and played indolently

slowly downward in remote
subterranean shaft
a diamond-tipped
drillpoint crept closer
to residual chaos to
rare artesian hatred
that once squirted warm
blood in God's face
confirming His first
disappointment in Eden

Nsukka, November 19, 1971

13

Benin Road

speed is violence
power is violence
weight violence

the butterfly
seeks safety
in lightness
in weightless
fluctuating flight

but somewhere
our divergent
territories meet
in paved forest tunnels

I come power-packed enough
for two and the gentle
butterfly pops open

in a bright yellow
smear in the silicon
hardness of my vision

December 9, 1971

Mango Seedling

Through glass window pane
Up a modern office block
I saw, two floors below, on wide-jutting
concrete canopy a mango seedling newly sprouted
Purple, two-leafed, standing on its burst
Black yolk. It waved brightly to sun and wind
Between rains—daily regaling itself
On seed-yams, prodigally.
For how long?
How long the happy waving
From precipice of rainswept sarcophagus?
How long the feast on remnant flour
At pot bottom?
　　　Perhaps like the widow
Of infinite faith it stood in wait
For the holy man of the forest, shaggy-haired
Powered for eternal replenishment.
Or else it hoped for Old Tortoise's miraculous feast

On one ever recurring dot of cocoyam
Set in a large bowl of green vegetables—
This day beyond fable, beyond faith?
    Then I saw it
Poised in courageous impartiality
Between the primordial quarrel of Earth
And Sky striving bravely to sink roots
Into objectivity, mid-air in stone.

I thought the rain, prime mover
To this enterprise, someday would rise in power
And deliver its ward in delirious waterfall
Toward earth below. But every rainy day
Little playful floods assembled on the slab,
Danced, parted round its feet,
United again, and passed.
It went from purple to sickly green
Before it died.
    Today I see it still—
Dry, wire-thin in sun and dust of the dry months—
Headstone on tiny debris of passionate courage.

Aba, 1968

The Explorer

Like a dawn unheralded at midnight
it opened abruptly before me—a rough
circular clearing, high cliffs of deep
forest guarding it in amber-tinted spell

A long journey's end it was though how
long and from where seemed unclear,
unimportant; one fact alone mattered
now—that body so well preserved
which on seeing I knew had brought me there

The circumstance of death
was vague but a floating hint
pointed to a disaster in the air
elusively

But where, if so, the litter
of violent wreckage? That rough-edged

gypsum trough bearing it like a dead
chrysalis reposing till now in full
encapsulation was broken by a cool
hand for this lying in state. All else
was in order except the leg missing
neatly at knee-joint
even the white schoolboy dress
immaculate in the thin yellow
light; the face in particular
was perfect having caught nor fear
nor agony at the fatal moment.

Clear-sighted with a clarity
rarely encountered in dreams
my Explorer-Self stood a little
distant but somewhat fulfilled; behind
him a long misty quest: unanswered
questions put to sleep needing
no longer to be raised. Enough
in that trapped silence of a freak
dawn to come face to face suddenly
with a body I didn't even know
I lost.

POEMS ABOUT WAR

The First Shot

That lone rifle-shot anonymous
in the dark striding chest-high
through a nervous suburb at the break
of our season of thunders will yet
steep its flight and lodge
more firmly than the greater noises
ahead in the forehead of memory.

Refugee Mother and Child

No Madonna and Child could touch
that picture of a mother's tenderness
for a son she soon would have to forget.

The air was heavy with odours
of diarrhoea of unwashed children
with washed-out ribs and dried-up
bottoms struggling in laboured
steps behind blown empty bellies. Most
mothers there had long ceased
to care but not this one; she held
a ghost smile between her teeth
and in her eyes the ghost of a mother's
pride as she combed the rust-coloured
hair left on his skull and then—
singing in her eyes—began carefully
to part it . . . In another life this
must have been a little daily

act of no consequence before his
breakfast and school; now she
did it like putting flowers
on a tiny grave.

Christmas in Biafra (1969)

This sunken-eyed moment wobbling
down the rocky steepness on broken
bones slowly fearfully to hideous
concourse of gathering sorrows in the valley
will yet become in another year a lost
Christmas irretrievable in the heights
its exploding inferno transmuted
by cosmic distances to the peacefulness
of a cool twinkling star . . . To death-cells
of that moment came faraway sounds of other
men's carols floating on crackling waves
mocking us. With regret? Hope? Longing? None of
these, strangely, not even despair rather
distilling pure transcendental hate . . .

Beyond the hospital gate
the good nuns had set up a manger
of palms to house a fine plastercast

scene at Bethlehem. The Holy
Family was central, serene, the Child
Jesus plump wise-looking and rose-cheeked; one
of the magi in keeping with legend
a black Othello in sumptuous robes. Other
figures of men and angels stood
at well-appointed distances from
the heart of the divine miracle
and the usual cattle gazed on
in holy wonder . . .

Poorer than the poor worshippers
before her who had paid their homage
with pitiful offering of new aluminium
coins that few traders would take and
a frayed five-shilling note she only
crossed herself and prayed open-eyed. Her
infant son flat like a dead lizard
on her shoulder his arms and legs
cauterized by famine was a miracle
of its kind. Large sunken eyes
stricken past boredom to a flat
unrecognizing glueyiness moped faraway
motionless across her shoulder . . .

Now her adoration over
she turned him around and pointed
at those pretty figures of God
and angels and men and beasts—
a spectacle to stir the heart
of a child. But all he vouchsafed
was one slow deadpan look of total

unrecognition and he began again
to swivel his enormous head away
to mope as before at his empty distance . . .
She shrugged her shoulders, crossed
herself again and took him away.

Air Raid

It comes so quickly
the bird of death
from evil forests of Soviet technology

A man crossing the road
to greet a friend
is much too slow.
His friend cut in halves
has other worries now
than a friendly handshake
at noon.

An "If" of History

Just think, had Hitler won
his war the mess our history
books would be today. The Americans
flushed by verdict of victory
hanged a Japanese commander for
war crimes. A generation later
an itching finger pokes their ribs:

     We've got to hang
     our Westmoreland
     for bloodier crimes
     in Viet Nam!

But everyone by now must
know that hanging takes much more
than a victim no matter his
load of manifest guilt. For even
in lynching a judge is needed—
a winner. Just think if Hitler
had gambled and won what chaos

the world would have known. His
implacable foe across the Channel
would surely have died for
war crimes. And as for H. Truman,
the Hiroshima villain, well!
Had Hitler won his war
De Gaulle would have needed no
further trial for was he not
condemned already by Paris
to die for his treason
to France? . . . Had Hitler won,
Vidkun Quisling would have kept
his job as Prime Minister
of Norway, simply by
Hitler winning.

Remembrance Day

Your proclaimed mourning
your flag at halfmast your
solemn face your smart backward
step and salute at the flowered
foot of empty graves your
glorious words—none, nothing
will their spirit appease. Had they
the choice they would gladly
have worn for you the same
stricken face gladly flown
your droopéd flag spoken
your tremulous eulogy—and
been alive . . . Admittedly you
suffered too. You lived wretchedly
on all manner of gross fare;
you were tethered to the nervous
precipice day and night; your
groomed hair lost gloss, your

smooth body roundedness. Truly
you suffered much. But now
you have the choice of a dozen
ways to rehabilitate yourself.
Pick any one of them and soon
you will forget the fear
and hardship, the peril
on the edge of the chasm . . . The
shops stock again a variety
of hair-dyes, the lace and
the gold are coming back; so
you will regain lost mirth
and girth and forget. But when,
how soon, will they their death? Long,
long after you forget they turned
newcomers again before the hazards
and rigours of reincarnation, rude
clods once more who once had borne
the finest scarifications of the potter's
delicate hand now squashed back
into primeval mud, they will
remember. Therefore fear them! Fear
their malice your fallen kindred
wronged in death. Fear their blood-feud;
tremble for the day of their
visit! Flee! Flee! Flee your
guilt palaces and cities! Flee
lest they come to ransack
your place and find you still
at home at the crossroad hour. Pray
that they return empty-handed
that day to nurse their red-hot

hatred for another long year . . .
your glorious words are not
for them nor your proliferation
in a dozen cities of the bronze
heroes of Idumota . . . Flee! Seek
asylum in distant places till
a new generation of heroes rise
in phalanges behind their purified
child-priest to inaugurate
a season of atonement and rescue
from fingers calloused by heavy deeds
the tender rites of reconciliation

After a War

After a war life catches
desperately at passing
hints of normalcy like
vines entwining a hollow
twig; its famished roots
close on rubble and every
piece of broken glass.

Irritations we used
to curse return to joyous
tables like prodigals home
from the city . . . The metre-man
serving my maiden bill brought
a friendly face to my circle
of sullen strangers and me
smiling gratefully
to the door.

After a war
we clutch at watery
scum pulsating on listless
eddies of our spent
deluge . . . Convalescent
dancers rising too soon
to rejoin their circle dance
our powerless feet intent
as before but no longer
adept contrive only
half-remembered
eccentric steps.

After years
of pressing death
and dizzy last-hour reprieves
we're glad to dump our fears
and our perilous gains together
in one shallow grave and flee
the same rueful way we came
straight home to haunted revelry.

Christmas 1971

POEMS NOT ABOUT WAR

Love Song (for Anna)

Bear with me my love
in the hour of my silence;
the air is criss-crossed
by loud omens and songbirds
fearing reprisals of middleday
have hidden away their notes
wrapped up in leaves
of cocoyam . . . What song shall I
sing to you my love when
a choir of squatting toads
turns the stomach of day with
goitrous adoration of an infested
swamp and purple-headed
vultures at home stand
sentry on the roof-top?

I will sing only in waiting
silence your power to bear

my dream for me in your quiet
eyes and wrap the dust of our blistered
feet in golden anklets ready
for the return someday of our
banished dance.

Love Cycle

At dawn slowly
the Sun withdraws his
long misty arms of
embrace. Happy lovers
whose exertions leave
no aftertaste nor slush
of love's combustion; Earth
perfumed in dewdrop
fragrance wakes
to whispers of
soft-eyed light . . .
     Later he
will wear out his temper
ploughing the vast acres
of heaven and take it
out of her in burning
darts of anger. Long
accustomed to such caprice

she waits patiently
for evening when thoughts
of another night will
restore his mellowness
and her power
over him.

Question

Angled sunbeam lowered
like Jacob's ladder through
sky's peep-hole pierced in the roof
to my silent floor and bared feet.
Are these your creatures
these crowding specks
stomping your lighted corridor
to a remote sun, like doped
acrobatic angels gyrating
at needlepoint to divert a high
unamused god? Or am I
sole stranger in a twilight room
I called my own overrun
and possessed long ago by myriads more
as yet invisible in all
this surrounding penumbra?

Answer

I broke at last
the terror-fringed fascination
that bound my ancient gaze
to those crowding faces
of plunder and seized my
remnant life in a miracle
of decision between white
collar hands and shook it
like a cheap watch in
my ear and threw it down
beside me on the earth floor
and rose to my feet. I
made of their shoulders
and heads bobbing up and down
a new ladder and leaned
it on their sweating flanks
and ascended till mid-air
my hands so new to harshness

could grapple the roughness of a prickly
day and quench the source
that fed turbulence to their
feet. I made a dramatic
descent that day landing
backways into crouching shadows
into potsherds of broken trance. I
flung open long-disused windows
and doors and saw my hut
new-swept by rainbow brooms
of sunlight become my home again
on whose trysting floor waited
my proud vibrant life.

Beware, Soul Brother

We are the men of soul
men of song we measure out
our joys and agonies
too, our long, long passion week
in paces of the dance. We have
come to know from surfeit of suffering
that even the Cross need not be
a dead end nor total loss
if we should go to it striding
the dirge of the soulful *abia* drums . . .

    But beware soul brother
of the lures of ascension day
the day of soporific levitation
on high winds of skysong; beware
for others there will be that day
lying in wait leaden-footed, tone-deaf
passionate only for the deep entrails
of our soil; beware of the day

we head truly skyward leaving
that spoil to the long ravenous tooth
and talon of their hunger.
Our ancestors, soul brother, were wiser
than is often made out. Remember
they gave Ala, great goddess
of their earth, sovereignty too over
their arts for they understood
so well those hard-headed
men of departed dance where a man's
foot must return whatever beauties
it may weave in air, where
it must return for safety
and renewal of strength. Take care
then, mother's son, lest you become
a dancer disinherited in mid-dance
hanging a lame foot in air like the hen
in a strange unfamiliar compound. Pray
protect this patrimony to which
you must return when the song
is finished and the dancers disperse;
remember also your children
for they in their time will want
a place for their feet when
they come of age and the dance
of the future is born
for them.

NON-*commitment*

Hurrah! to them who do nothing
see nothing feel nothing whose
hearts are fitted with prudence
like a diaphragm across
womb's beckoning doorway to bar
the scandal of seminal rage. I'm
told the owl too wears wisdom
in a ring of defence round
each vulnerable eye securing it fast
against the darts of sight. Long ago
in the Middle East Pontius Pilate
openly washed involvement off his
white hands and became famous. (Of all
the Roman officials before him and after
who else is talked about
every Sunday in the Apostles' Creed?) And
talking of apostles that other fellow
Judas wasn't such a fool

either; though much maligned by
succeeding generations the fact remains
he alone in that motley crowd
had sense enough to tell a doomed
movement when he saw one
and get out quick, a nice little
packet bulging his coat-pocket
into the bargain—sensible fellow.

September 1970

Generation Gap

A son's arrival
is the crescent moon
too new too soon to lodge
the man's returning. His
feast of re-incarnation
must await the moon's
ripening at the naming
ceremony of his
grandson.

Misunderstanding

My old man had a little saying
he loved and as he neared
his end was prone to relish
more and more. Wherever Something
stands, he'd say, there also Something
Else will stand. Heedless at first
I waved it aside as mere
elderly prattle that youth have to bear
till sharply one day it hit home to me
that never before, not even
once, did I hear mother speak
again in their little disputes once
he'd said it. From then began
my long unrest: what was this
Thing so unanswerable and why
was it dogged by that
relentless Other? My mother
proved no help at all nor did

my father whose sole reply
was just a solemn smile . . . Quietly
later of its own will it showed
its face, so slowly, to me though
not before they'd long been dead—my
little old man and my mother
also—and showed me too how
utterly vain my private quest
had been. Flushed by success
I spoke one day in a trifling
row: you see, my darling (to
my wife) where Something
stands—no matter what—there
Something Else will take its
stand. I knew, she said; she
pouted her lips like a gun
in my face. She knew, she said,
she'd known all along of that
other woman I was keeping in town.
And I fear, my friends,
I am yet to hear
the last of it.

Bull and Egret

At seventy miles an hour
one morning down the see-saw
road to Nsukka I came
upon a mighty bull
in form and carriage
so unlike Fulani cattle—
gaunt, high-horned, triangular
faced—that come in herded
multitudes from dusty savannahs
to the north . . . Heavy
was he, solitary dark
and taciturn, one of a tribe
they say fate has chosen
for slow extinction. At his heels
paced his egret, intent
praise-singer, pure white
all neck, walking high
stilts and yet no higher

than his master's leg-joint . . .
Odd covetousness indeed would
leave its boundless green estates
for a spell of petty trespassing
on perilous asphalt laid for me! . . . My
frantic blast of iron voice
shattered their stately march, then
recoiled brutally to my heart
as he gathered in hasty panic
the heaviness of his hind-
quarters, so ungainly in his
hurry, and flung it desperate
beyond my monstrous
reach. I should have felt unworthy then
playing such pranks on the noble
elder and watching his hallowed
waist-cloth come undone had not
his singer fared so well . . . Two
quick hops, a flap of
wings and he was
safe posture intact on
brown laterite . . . I could not
bear him playing so
faithfully my faithless agility-man, my
scrambler to safety, throat dilated
still by remnant praises
of his excellency high-headed
in delusion marching now alone
into death's ambush . . . We were
spared, the bull and I, in our separate follies . . .
His routed sunrise procession
no doubt would reform beyond the clamour

of my passage and sprightly
egret take up again
his broken adulation
of the bull, his everlasting
prince, his giver-in-abundance
of heavenly cattle-ticks.

Lazarus

We know the breath-taking
joy of his sisters when the word
spread: He is risen! But a
man who has lived a full life
will have others to
reckon with beside his
sisters. Certainly that keen-eyed
subordinate who has moved up
to his table at the office, for
him resurrection is an awful
embarrassment . . . The luckless
people of Ogbaku knew its
terrors that day the twin-headed
evil strode their highway. It
could not have been easy
picking up again the blood-spattered
clubs they had cast away; or to
turn from the battered body

of the barrister lying beside his
battered limousine to finish off
their own man, stirring now suddenly
in wide-eyed resurrection . . . How well
they understood, those grim-faced
villagers wielding their crimson
weapons once more, that at the hour
of his rising their kinsman
avenged in murder would turn
away from them in obedience
to other fraternities, would turn indeed
their own accuser and in one
breath obliterate their plea
and justification! So they killed
him a second time that day on the
threshold of a promising resurrection.

Vultures

In the greyness
and drizzle of one despondent
dawn unstirred by harbingers
of sunbreak a vulture
perching high on broken
bone of a dead tree
nestled close to his
mate his smooth
bashed-in head, a pebble
on a stem rooted in
a dump of gross
feathers, inclined affectionately
to hers. Yesterday they picked
the eyes of a swollen
corpse in a water-logged
trench and ate the
things in its bowel. Full
gorged they chose their roost
keeping the hollowed remnant

in easy range of cold
telescopic eyes . . .
                    Strange
indeed how love in other
ways so particular
will pick a corner
in that charnel-house
tidy it and coil up there, perhaps
even fall asleep—her face
turned to the wall!
. . . Thus the Commandant at Belsen
Camp going home for
the day with fumes of
human roast clinging
rebelliously to his hairy
nostrils will stop
at the wayside sweet-shop
and pick up a chocolate
for his tender offspring
waiting at home for Daddy's
return . . .
        Praise bounteous
providence if you will
that grants even an ogre
a tiny glow-worm
tenderness encapsulated
in icy caverns of a cruel
heart or else despair
for in the very germ
of that kindred love is
lodged the perpetuity
of evil.

Public Execution in Pictures

The caption did not overlook
the smart attire of the squad. Certainly
there was impressive swagger in that
ready, high-elbowed stance; belted
and sashed in threaded dragon teeth
they waited in self-imposed restraint—
fine ornament on power unassailable—
for their cue

        at the crucial time
this pretty close-up lady in fine lace
proved unequal to it, her first no doubt,
and quickly turned away. But not
this other—her face, rigid
in pain, firmly held between her palms;
though not perfect yet, it seems
clear she has put the worst
behind her today

                    in my home
far from the crowded live-show
on the hot, bleached sands of Victoria
Beach my little kids will crowd
round our Sunday paper and debate
hotly why the heads of dead
robbers always slump forwards
or sideways.

GODS, MEN AND OTHERS

Penalty of Godhead

The old man's bed
of straw caught a flame blown
from overnight logs by harmattan's
incendiary breath. Defying his age and
sickness he rose and steered himself
smoke-blind to safety.

A nimble rat appeared at the
door of his hole looked quickly to left and
right and scurried across the floor
to nearby farmlands.

Even roaches that grim
tenantry that nothing discourages
fled their crevices that day on wings they
only use in deadly haste.

Household gods alone
frozen in ritual black with blood
of endless tribute festooned in feathers
perished in the blazing pyre
of that hut.

Those Gods Are Children

No man who loves himself
will dare to drink
before his fathers' presences enshrined
by the threshold have drunk
their fill. A fool alone will
contest the precedence of ancestors
and gods; the wise wisely
sing them grandiloquent lullabies
knowing they are children
those omnipotent deities.
Take that avid-eyed old man
full horn in veined hand
unsteadied by age who calls
forward his fathers tilting the horn
with amazing skill for a hand
so tremulous till grudging trickles
break through white froth
at the brim and course down

the curved side to fine point
of sacrifice ant-hole-size in earth:
>   come together all-powerful spirits
>   and drink; no need to scramble
>   there's enough for all!
Or when the offering of yams
is due who sends the lively
errand son to scour the barn
and bring a sacrifice fit
for the mighty dead! Naive
eager to excel the child
returns in sweat lumbering
the heavy pride of his father's harvest:
>   ignorant child, all ears and no eyes!
>   is that the biggest in my barn?
>   I said the biggest!
Only then does the nimble child
perceive a surreptitious fist quickly shown
and withdrawn again—and break through
wisdom's lashing cordon to welcoming smiles
of initiation. He makes the journey
of the neophyte to bring home a ritual
offering as big as an egg.

II

Long ago a man of fury drawn
by doom's insistent call slew
his brother. The land and all its deities
screamed revenge: a head for a head
and raised their spear
to smite the town should it
withhold the due. The man
was ready. The elders' council
looked at him and turned
from him to all the orphans doubly
doomed and shook their heads:
    the gods are right and just! This man
    shall hang but first may he
    retrieve the sagging house
    of his fathers

and the fine points
of the gods' spears
returned to earth

and he lived for years that man
of death he raised his orphans
he worked his homestead and his farmlands
till evening came and laid him low
with cruel foraging fever. Patient
elders peering through the hut's dim
light darkened more by smoke
of smouldering fire under his bed
steady-eyed at a guilt they had stalked
across scrublands and seven rivers, a long-prepared
hangman's loop in their hand
quickly circled his neck
as he died

and the gods
and ancestors
were satisfied.

III

They are strong and to be feared
they make the mighty crash
in ruin like iroko's fall
at height of noon scattering
nests and frantic birdsong
in damped silence of deep
undergrowth. Yet they are fooled
as easily as children those deities
their simple omnipotence
drowsed by praise.

Lament of the Sacred Python

I was there when lizards
were ones and twos, child
Of sacred father Idemili. Painful
Tear-drops of Sky's first weeping
Drew my spots. Sky-born
I walked the earth with royal gait
And crowds of human mourners
Filing down funereal paths
Across lengthening shadows
Of the dead acknowledged my face
In broken dirges of fear.

But of late
A wandering god pursued,
It seems, by hideous things
He did at home has come to us
And pitched his tent here
Beneath the people's holy tree

And hoisted from its pinnacle
A charlatan bell that calls
Unknown monotones of revolts,
Scandals, and false immunities.
And I that none before could meet except
In fear though I brought no terrors
From creation's day of gifts I must now
Turn on my track
In dishonourable flight
Where children stop their play
To shriek in my ringing ears:
  Look out, python! Look out, python!
  Christians relish python flesh!

And great father Idemili
That once upheld from earth foundations
Cloud banks of sky's endless waters
Is betrayed in his shrine by empty men
Suborned with the stranger's tawdry gifts
And taken trussed up to the altar-shrine turned
Slaughter house for the gory advent
Feast of an errant cannibal god
Tooth-filed to eat his fellows.

And the sky recedes in
Anger; the orphan snake
Abandoned weeps in the shadows.

Their Idiot Song

These fellows, the old pagan
said, surely are out of their mind—
that old proudly impervious
derelict skirted long ago by floodwaters
of salvation: Behold the great
and gory handiwork of Death displayed
for all on dazzling sheets this
hour of day its twin nostrils
plugged firmly with stoppers of wool
and they ask of him: Where
is thy sting?

        Sing on, good fellows, sing
on! Someday when it is you
he decks out on his great
iron-bed with cotton-wool
for your breath, his massing odours
mocking your pitiful makeshift defences
of face powder and township ladies' lascivious

scent, these others roaming
yet his roomy chicken-coop will
be singing and asking still
but you by then
no longer will be
in doubt!

EPILOGUE

He Loves Me; He Loves Me Not*

"Harold Wilson he loves
me he gave me
a gun in my time
of need to shoot
my rebellious brother. Edward
Heath he loves
me not he's promised a gun
to his sharp-shooting
brother viewing me
crazily through ramparts
of white Pretoria . . . It
would be awful
if he got me." It was
awful and he got
him. They headlined it
on the BBC spreading

* Lines provoked by the news that a street in Port Harcourt has been named
after Harold Wilson.

indignation through the
world, later that day
in emergency meeting his
good friend Wilson and Heath
his enemy crossed swords
over him at West-
minster and sent post-
haste Sir Alec to Africa
for the funeral.

Dereliction

I quit the carved stool
in my father's hut to the swelling
chant of sabre-tooth termites
raising in the pith of its wood
a white-bellied stalagmite

Where does a runner go
whose oily grip drops
the baton handed by the faithful one
in a hard, merciless race? Or
the priestly elder who barters
for the curio collector's head
of tobacco the holy staff
of his people?

Let them try the land
where the sea retreats
Let them try the land
where the sea retreats

We Laughed at Him

We laughed at him our
hungry-eyed fool-man with itching
fingers who would see farther
than all. We called him
visionary missionary revolutionary
and, you know, all the other
naries that plague the peace, but
nothing would deter him.

With his own nails he cut
his eyes, scraped the crust
over them peeled off his priceless
patina of rest and the dormant
fury of his dammed pond
broke into a cataract
of blood tumbling down
his face and chest . . . We
laughed at his screams the fool-man

who would see what eyes
are forbidden, the hungry-eyed
man, the look-look man, the
itching man bent to drag
into daylight fearful signs
hidden away for our safety
at the creation of the world.

He was always against
blindness, you know, our quiet
sober blindness, our lazy—he called
it—blindness. And for
his pains? A turbulent, torrential
cascading blindness behind
a Congo river of blood. He sat
backstage then behind his flaming red
curtain and groaned in
the pain his fingers unlocked, in the
rainstorm of blows loosed on his head
by the wild avenging demons he
drummed free from the silence of their
drum-house, his prize for big-eyed greed.
We sought by laughter to
drown his anguish . . . But suddenly
one day at height of noon his
screams turned to hymns of
ecstacy. We knew then his
pain had risen to the
brain and we took pity
on him the poor fool-man
as he held converse with
himself. We heard him say:

"My lord" to the curtain
of his blood, "I come to
touch the hem of your crimson
robe." He went stark mad thereafter
raving about new sights he
claimed to see, poor fellow; sights
you and I know are as impossible for this world
to show as for a hen to urinate—if one
may borrow one of his many crazy vulgarisms—
he raved about trees topped with
green and birds flying—yes actually
flying through the air—about
the sun and the moon and stars
and about lizards crawling on all
fours . . . But nobody worries much
about him today; he has paid
his price and we don't even
bother to laugh any more.

NOTES

MANGO SEEDLING

LINE 14: *the widow of infinite faith* refers to the story of the widow of Sarephath in the First Book of Kings, Chapter 17.

LINE 18: *Old Tortoise's miraculous feast*: Once upon a time Tortoise went to work for an old woman and at the end of his labours she set before him a bowl containing a lone cocoyam sitting on a mound of cooked green leaves. Naturally Tortoise protested vehemently and refused to touch such a meagre meal. In the end, however, he was persuaded, still protesting, to eat it. Then he discovered to his amazement (and nearly his undoing) that another cocoyam always appeared in the bowl as soon as he ate the last one.

LINE 24: *the primordial quarrel of Earth and Sky*. This was a dispute over who was sovereign. It led finally to Sky's withholding of rain for seven whole years, until the ground became hard as iron and the dead could not be buried. Only then did Earth sue for peace, sending high-flying Vulture as emissary.

CHRISTMAS IN BIAFRA (1969)

LINE 30: *new aluminium coins.* A completely unsuccessful effort was made in Biafra to peg galloping prices by introducing new coins of a lower denomination than the paper money that had come in earlier. But it was too late. The market having already settled for the five-shilling currency-note as its smallest medium of exchange paid no heed to the new coins which simply fizzled out.

AN "IF" OF HISTORY

LINE 5: A Japanese General named Tomayuki Yamashita was hanged by the Americans at the end of the Second World War for war crimes committed by troops under his nominal command in the Philippines.

REMEMBRANCE DAY

The Igbo people around my home-town, Ogidi, had an annual observance called Ọsọ Nwanadi. On the night preceding it all able-bodied men in the village took flight and went into hiding in neighbouring villages in order to escape the ire of Nwanadi or dead kindred killed in war.

Although the Igbo people admire courage and valour they do not glamourize death, least of all death in battle. They have no valhalla concept; the dead hero bears the living a grudge. Life is the "natural" state; death is tolerable only when it leads again to life—to reincarnation. Two sayings of the Igbo will illustrate their attitude to death:

(a) a person who cries because he is sick what will they do who are dead?

(b) Before a dead man is reincarnated an emaciated man will recover his flesh.

LOVE SONG (FOR ANNA)

LINE 7: leaves of cocoyam come in handy for wrapping small and delicate things. For instance, before storage kola nuts are wrapped in cocoyam leaves to preserve them from desiccation. However, cocoyam leaves are not for roughhandling as Vulture learnt to his cost when he received from the hands of an appeased Sky a bundle of rain wrapped in them to take home to drought-stricken Earth.

BEWARE, SOUL BROTHER

LINE 10: *abia* drums beaten at the funeral of an Igbo titled man. The dance itself is also called *abia* and is danced by the dead man's peers while he lies in state and finally by two men bearing his coffin before it is taken for burial; so he goes to his ancestors by a final *rite de passage* in solemn paces of dance.

MISUNDERSTANDING

The Igbo people have a firm belief in the duality of things. Nothing is by itself, nothing is absolute. "I am the way, the Truth and the Life" would be meaningless in Igbo theology. They say that man may be right by Udo and yet be killed by Ogwugwu; in other words, he may worship one god to perfection and yet fall foul of another.

Igbo proverbs bring out this duality of existence very well. Take any proverb which puts forward a point of view or a "truth" and you can always find another that contradicts it or at least puts a limitation on the absoluteness of its validity.

LAZARUS

LINE 12: *Ogbaku:* Many years ago a strange and terrible thing happened in the small village of Ogbaku. A lawyer driving through the highway that passes by that village ran over a man. The villagers, thinking the man was killed, set upon the lawyer and clubbed him to death. Then to their horror, their man began to stir. So, the story went, they set upon him too and finished him off, saying, "You can't come back having made us do that."

THOSE GODS ARE CHILDREN

The attitude of Igbo people to their gods is sometimes ambivalent. This arises from a world-view which sees the land of the spirits as a territorial extension of the human domain. Each sphere has its functions as well as its privileges in relation to the other. Thus a man is not entirely without authority in dealing with the spirit-world nor entirely at its mercy. The deified spirits of his ancestors look after his welfare; in return he offers them sustenance regularly in the form of sacrifice. In such a reciprocal relationship one is encouraged (within reason) to try and get the better of the bargain.

LAMENT OF THE SACRED PYTHON

LINE 10: *acknowledged my face in broken dirges*. One of the songs that accompany the dead to the burial place at nightfall has these lines:

> Look a python! Look a python!
> Python lies across the way!

LINE 24: *creation's day of gifts*. We all choose our gifts, our character, our fate from the Creator just before we make our journey into the world. The sacred python did not choose (like some other snakes) the terror of the fang and venom and yet it received a presence more overpowering than theirs.

THEIR IDIOT SONG

The christian claim of victory over death is to the unconverted villager one of the really puzzling things about the faith. Are these christians just naive or plain hypocritical?

DERELICTION

This poem is in three short movements. The first is the enquirer
(onye ajụjụ); the second the mediating diviner (dibia) who frames
the enquiry in general terms and the third is the Oracle.

WE LAUGHED AT HIM

LINE 36: *wild avenging demons*. This refers to the story of Tortoise
and the miraculous food-drum offered him in spirit-land in
return for his palm-nut that one of the spirit-children has
eaten. After long use (and misuse) the drum ceases to produce
any more feasts when it is beaten. Whereupon Tortoise
blatantly contrives a re-enactment of his first visit to spirit-land.
But this time the spirits (fully aware no doubt, of his greed)
take him to a long row of hanging drums and allow him to
pick one for himself. As you would expect he picks the largest
and lumbers away under its great weight. Home at last he
makes elaborate arrangements for a feast and then beats the
drum. No food comes, instead demons armed with long whips
emerge and belabour him to their satisfaction.

The element of choice is a recurrent theme in Igbo thought
especially in man's dealings with the spirit-world. We are not
forced; we make a free choice.